Zodiac Leaves

Zodiac Leaves

Aligning the Stars

Matthew Petchinsky

Apophis Enterprises LLC

Zodiac Leaves: Aligning the Stars
By: Matthew Petchinsky

Introduction 1A

Astrology has been a fascination for thousands of years, there are many different versions of it and it has had the hearts and mind of man in every culture on Earth, since mankind was primitive Caveman in a cave to Egyptian to modern man. Astrology is engrained in our DNA. Please enjoy this book.

Introduction 2B

In the vast expanse of the universe, where celestial bodies orchestrate the dance of life, there lies an ancient wisdom that binds the heavens to the Earth—astrology. Parallelly, the Earth nurtures a verdant realm of flora, each plant pulsating with unique vibrational energies. "Zodiac Leaves: Aligning the Stars" emerges as a harmonious blend of these two mystical worlds, intending to bridge the celestial with the terrestrial. This guide is a testament to the belief that the wisdom of the stars, when combined with the healing essence of plants, can offer profound insights and transformative experiences. Our purpose and vision is to unveil the symbiotic relationship between the zodiac signs and plants, illuminating paths to personal growth, wellness, and a deeper connection with the cosmos.

Astrology and Plants: An Interconnected Universe

Astrology, the language of the stars, and botany, the study of plants, might seem worlds apart, yet they share a common thread—energy. Every zodiac sign emanates specific vibrational energies, reflecting traits, emotions, and tendencies. Similarly, plants possess unique vibrations, imbued with the capacity to heal, invigorate, and balance. This guide explores the mystical linkage between the twelve zodiac signs and the botanical world, uncovering how certain plants resonate with specific astrological energies. By understanding this connection, one can harness the power of plants to amplify the positive aspects of their zodiac sign, mitigate challenges, and foster a harmonious balance within.

Navigating the Guide: A Journey of Self-Discovery and Harmony
"Zodiac Leaves: Aligning the Stars" is more than a book; it's a journey towards self-discovery, healing, and cosmic alignment. To navigate this guide:

- **Personal Growth**: Embark on a journey to understand the intrinsic connection between your zodiac sign and its corresponding plants. Discover how these plants can influence your personal growth, aiding in self-reflection, enhancing strengths, and addressing areas of improvement.

- **Healing Practices**: Explore the healing virtues of plants aligned with your zodiac sign. From herbal teas to essential oils, learn how to incorporate these plants into your daily practices for physical, emotional, and spiritual healing.

- **Aligning with Cosmic Energies**: This guide offers insights into the dynamic energies of the cosmos and how they interact with the vibrational frequencies of plants. Learn to align your energy with the cosmic flow, optimizing times for action, reflection, and rest according to the celestial calendar.

"Zodiac Leaves: Aligning the Stars" is an invitation to those who seek harmony between their inner world and the cosmic forces that pervade the universe. It is a call to blend the ancient wisdom of astrology with the healing power of plants, embarking on a transformative journey that aligns the stars with the essence of life itself.

Chapter 1: Astrology and Herbalism - An Ancient Connection
Historical Context: Tracing back the Historical Ties

The convergence of astrology and herbalism is not a novel concept; rather, it is a revival of ancient wisdom that has been intertwined with human history for millennia. Our ancestors observed the heavens and the earth with reverence, recognizing patterns and cycles in the cosmos that mirrored the rhythms of life on Earth. Astrology, the study of the movements and relative positions of celestial bodies interpreted as having an influence on human affairs and the natural world, served as a guide for living in harmony with these cosmic energies. Concurrently, herbalism, the practice of using plants for healing, emerged from a deep understanding of the natural world, recognizing that each herb carried its own unique energy and purpose.

Ancient civilizations such as the Egyptians, Greeks, Chinese, and Indians independently discovered connections between the stars and the medicinal properties of plants. They documented these relationships, using celestial events to guide their agricultural and healing practices. The Greek physician Hippocrates, often regarded as the father of medicine, famously stated, "He who does not understand astrology is not a doctor but a fool." This exemplifies the integral role astrology played in ancient healing practices, where the alignment of the planets was considered vital in diagnosing and treating illnesses.

The Foundation of Energies: Understanding How Energies Work

At the heart of the connection between astrology and herbalism lies the concept of energy. In astrology, celestial bodies are believed to emit energies that influence the characteristics of individuals born under certain zodiac signs, as well as the physical and emotional states of all living beings. Similarly, plants are viewed as living entities imbued with their own distinct energies, capable of influencing the human body and spirit.

This shared foundation is based on the principle of vibrational energy, which posits that everything in the universe vibrates at different frequencies. These vibrations create patterns that can harmonize or discord with one another. The art of astrology and herbalism, then, is the practice of understanding and aligning these vibrational energies to promote healing and balance.

Practical Applications: Introducing Ways to Apply These Connections in Modern Healing Practices

Today, the ancient connection between astrology and herbalism is experiencing a renaissance, as people seek more holistic approaches to health and wellness. This revival emphasizes not just physical healing, but emotional and spiritual well-being. Here are some ways to apply these ancient connections in modern healing practices:

- **Herbal Remedies Based on Zodiac Signs**: By understanding the energetic properties of plants and how they correlate with the zodiac signs, practitioners can create personalized herbal remedies. For example, fiery Aries might benefit from calming herbs like lavender to balance their innate intensity, while earthy Taurus might find grounding in roots like dandelion.

- **Planting and Harvesting by the Moon**: The lunar cycle plays a crucial role in gardening and farming. By planting seeds, tending to crops, and harvesting herbs in alignment with the phases of the Moon, one can optimize the energetic qualities and medicinal properties of the plants.

- **Astrological Timing for Healing Rituals**: Timing healing rituals and practices according to astrological events, such as new moons, full moons, and planetary alignments, can enhance their effectiveness. This includes preparing herbal remedies, meditating, and performing cleansing rituals.

- **Energy Balancing Through Herbal Elixirs**: Creating elixirs, teas, and other concoctions with plants that align with an individual's sun, moon, and rising signs can help balance energy, address specific health concerns, and promote overall well-being.

"Zodiac Leaves: Aligning the Stars" aims to rekindle the sacred bond between astrology and herbalism, guiding readers through a journey of self-discovery, healing, and alignment with the cosmos. By embracing the ancient wisdom encapsulated in the stars and the earth, we can navigate the complexities of modern life with greater harmony and balance.

If you want to see some amazing products, please visit my Virtual Dispensary: https://shift.store/sg1fan23477/retail

Chapter 2: Preparing for Your Journey

Embarking on a journey of aligning with the cosmic energies through the wisdom of plants requires preparation, both of your physical space and your inner self. This chapter guides you through creating a sacred space, understanding your astrological blueprint via your natal chart, and selecting plants that resonate with your unique astrological makeup. This foundational work sets the stage for a harmonious journey of growth, healing, and self-discovery.

Creating Sacred Space

Creating a sacred space involves preparing both your physical environment and your mental state to engage deeply with the energies of astrology and herbalism. This space becomes your sanctuary for healing, learning, and growth.

- **Physical Space**: Choose a quiet, comfortable area where you can be uninterrupted. This could be a corner of a room, a garden, or any place where you feel at peace. Cleanse this space of negative energies by smudging with sage, palo santo, or using sound vibrations like bells or singing bowls. Consider placing items that hold personal significance or spiritual value around you, such as crystals, pictures, or symbols related to your zodiac sign.

- **Mental Space**: Preparing your mental space is equally important. Begin with grounding exercises, meditation, or deep breathing to center yourself. Setting intentions for your journey can help focus your energies and clarify your goals. Embrace openness and release any preconceived notions or expectations. This mental preparation allows you to be more receptive to the teachings of the stars and the wisdom of the earth.

Understanding Your Natal Chart

Your natal chart, a snapshot of the cosmos at the time of your birth, is a powerful tool for self-discovery. It reveals your strengths, challenges, and potential paths for growth. Understanding your chart is crucial for aligning with astrological energies.

- **Basic Components**: Familiarize yourself with the basic components of your natal chart—Sun sign, Moon sign, and Ascendant (or Rising sign). Each provides insight into different aspects of your personality and life experiences.

- **Planetary Positions**: Pay attention to the positions of the planets and their aspects to each other. These relationships highlight areas of life that are harmonious or challenging, guiding you towards areas where growth and healing are needed.

- **Houses and Signs**: The chart is divided into twelve houses, each representing a different area of life. The signs and planets within these houses offer detailed insights into your personal dynamics in these areas.

Selecting Your Plants

Choosing plants that resonate with your astrological makeup can enhance your connection to the cosmic energies and support your journey in unique ways. This intuitive process requires an open heart and mind.

- **Resonance with Zodiac Signs**: Each zodiac sign is associated with specific plants that embody the sign's energy. Start by exploring plants connected to your Sun, Moon, and Rising signs. Notice which plants you feel naturally drawn to or which ones intrigue you.

- **Intuitive Selection**: Beyond astrological associations, allow your intuition to guide you in selecting plants. Spend time in nature or a garden, touching, smelling, and observing different plants.

Trust your instincts on which plants you feel a deep connection with or which ones seem to call out to you.

- **Consider Your Needs**: Reflect on what you seek from this journey—be it healing, protection, clarity, or love. Select plants known for their properties that align with these desires. Remember, this selection process is deeply personal and fluid; your plant allies may change as you grow and evolve.

Preparing for your journey in "Zodiac Leaves: Aligning the Stars" is an essential step towards achieving harmony and balance within and with the universe. By creating a sacred space, understanding your natal chart, and intuitively selecting your plant allies, you lay a strong foundation for a transformative path of alignment with the stars.

If you want to see some amazing products, please visit my Virtual Dispensary: https://shift.store/sg1fan23477/retail

Chapter 3: Aries - The Pioneering Spirit
Aries Overview

Aries, the first sign of the zodiac, heralds the beginning of the astrological year, embodying the pioneering spirit of new beginnings. Ruled by Mars, the planet of energy and action, Aries individuals are known for their dynamic energy, courage, and determination. They are natural leaders, ready to blaze trails and take on challenges with a boldness that is both inspiring and intimidating.

Traits: Aries are characterized by their vibrant energy, assertiveness, and willingness to explore uncharted territories. They possess an innate confidence and a straightforward approach to life.

Strengths: Among their greatest strengths are leadership, courage, and an unwavering optimism. Aries have the unique ability to inspire others with their enthusiasm and zest for life.

Challenges: However, their fiery nature can sometimes lead to impulsiveness, impatience, and a tendency to start projects without finishing them. Learning to channel their abundant energy constructively is key for Aries to achieve their ambitious goals.

Herbal Allies for Aries

The fiery energy of Aries resonates with plants that embody courage, protection, and the power to ignite the warrior spirit within. These herbal allies can help balance Aries' intense energy, providing grounding and support for their boundless ambition.

- **Nettles (Urtica dioica)**: This herb fuels Aries' fiery energy, offering a rich source of nutrients to nourish their dynamic spirit. Nettles are known for their ability to purify the blood and enhance vitality, embodying the essence of courage and protection.
- **Ginger (Zingiber officinale)**: Ginger's warming and stimulating properties make it an excellent ally for Aries, igniting their digestive fire and boosting their natural vitality. It also helps in channeling their energy more effectively, reducing impulsiveness.
- **Rosemary (Rosmarinus officinalis)**: This herb resonates with the Mars-ruled Aries, enhancing mental clarity and focus, which are crucial for Aries to complete their pioneering projects. Rosemary also supports memory and concentration, empowering Aries in their leadership roles.
- **Peppermint (Mentha piperita)**: Peppermint offers a cooling counterbalance to Aries' hot and fiery nature, promoting calm and relaxation. It aids in digestion and soothes headaches, common ailments of those who live at Aries' fast pace.

Rituals and Practices

Creating a motivational morning tea ritual can help ignite Aries' dynamic nature, setting a positive tone for the day ahead. This ritual harnesses the power of Aries' herbal allies to fuel their pioneering spirit.

Morning Tea Ritual for Aries

1. **Prepare Your Space**: Begin by creating a calm environment where you can focus on your intentions for the day. Light a candle to symbolize the fire within you.
2. **Select Your Herbs**: Choose from your herbal allies—nettle for courage, ginger for vitality, rosemary for focus, and peppermint for balance. You can use them individually or create a blend tailored to your current needs.
3. **Set Your Intention**: As you prepare your tea, focus on your intention for the day. Whether it's tackling a new project, leading

a team, or simply finding balance, let this intention infuse with your tea.

4. **Sip and Visualize**: Drink your tea slowly, visualizing your intention manifesting throughout the day. Feel the herbs' energies fueling your spirit, enhancing your natural strengths, and addressing your challenges.

5. **Closing the Ritual**: Thank your herbal allies for their support. Carry the warmth and energy from your tea throughout your day, letting it inspire and motivate you in your endeavors.

This morning tea ritual for Aries is a powerful practice for starting the day with intention and vigor. By aligning with their herbal allies, Aries can harness their pioneering spirit to its fullest potential, turning challenges into opportunities for growth and leadership.

If you want to see some amazing products, please visit my Virtual Dispensary: https://shift.store/sg1fan23477/retail

Chapter 4: Taurus - The Earth's Blossom
Taurus Overview

Taurus, the second sign of the zodiac, is deeply connected to the earth and the material world. Ruled by Venus, the planet of love, beauty, and value, Taurus individuals are known for their dependability, sensuality, and a strong connection to the physical senses. Taureans are the embodiment of steadiness and persistence, moving through life with a calm and deliberate pace that mirrors the unfolding of nature itself.

Traits: Taureans are characterized by their love for comfort, beauty, and stability. They revel in the pleasures of life, finding joy in the simple things - a gourmet meal, a beautiful landscape, or the touch of luxurious fabric.

Strengths: Among their greatest strengths are loyalty, patience, and practicality. Taurus individuals build their lives on a foundation of reliability and hard work, creating enduring value in everything they do.

Challenges: However, their strong desire for stability can sometimes manifest as stubbornness and resistance to change. They may struggle with letting go and embracing new opportunities, preferring the safety of the familiar.

Herbal Allies for Taurus

For the earthy Taurus, herbal allies are those that encourage grounding, enhance relaxation, and soothe the stubborn streak, allowing for flexibility and openness to change.

- **Chamomile (Matricaria chamomilla)**: This herb is a balm for Taurus' sometimes stubborn nature, offering a gentle reminder to relax and let go. Chamomile promotes calmness and relaxation, easing stress and tension.
- **Lavender (Lavandula angustifolia)**: Lavender's soothing fragrance and properties help to ease the mind and body, encouraging a sense of peace and tranquility that can help Taurus individuals unwind and embrace a more flexible outlook.
- **Rose (Rosa spp.)**: Aligned with Venus, rose supports Taurus' sensual nature, nurturing the heart and fostering self-love and acceptance. It gently encourages openness to love and beauty in all forms.
- **Patchouli (Pogostemon cablin)**: Earthy and grounding, patchouli helps to deepen Taurus' connection to the earth, enhancing stability and grounding. It can help in balancing Taurus' practicality with a deeper spiritual awareness.

Rituals and Practices

A grounding garden meditation offers Taurus individuals a profound way to connect with the earth's energies, fostering a sense of stability while opening the heart and mind to change.

Grounding Garden Meditation for Taurus

1. **Prepare Your Space**: Choose a quiet spot in a garden or a place where you can be close to the earth. Remove your shoes to physically connect with the ground.
2. **Select Your Herbs**: Bring along a sachet of Taurus' herbal allies —chamomile, lavender, rose, and patchouli. Hold them in your

hands or place them nearby to infuse your meditation space with their grounding energies.

3. **Grounding Exercise**: Sit or stand comfortably, closing your eyes. Visualize roots extending from the soles of your feet or your base, going deep into the earth. Feel the stability and nourishment coming from this connection.

4. **Meditation and Reflection**: Focus on your breath, allowing each inhale to draw up the earth's energy, and each exhale to release any resistance to change or stubbornness. Reflect on the areas of your life where you might benefit from more flexibility and openness.

5. **Closing the Practice**: Thank the earth and your herbal allies for their support. Take a moment to acknowledge the beauty and abundance around you, embracing a sense of gratitude for the simple pleasures in life.

This grounding garden meditation helps Taurus individuals to strengthen their connection to the earth while encouraging a gentle openness to change. By engaging in this practice, Taureans can balance their need for stability with the natural flow of life, allowing them to blossom fully, like the earth they so cherish.

If you want to see some amazing products, please visit my Virtual Dispensary: https://shift.store/sg1fan23477/retail

Chapter 5: Gemini - The Cosmic Communicator

Gemini Overview

Gemini, the third sign of the zodiac, embodies the essence of communication, intellectual exploration, and adaptability. Ruled by Mercury, the planet of communication, Gemini individuals are curious, articulate, and enjoy exchanging ideas. They thrive on variety and are known for their quick wit and broad knowledge base.

Traits: Geminis are characterized by their sharp intellect, curiosity, and desire to explore new concepts. Their dual nature allows them to see both sides of any situation, making them excellent mediators and problem-solvers.

Strengths: Among their greatest strengths are versatility, adaptability, and the ability to communicate effectively. Geminis can easily navigate through different social circles, bringing lightness and humor wherever they go.

Challenges: However, their love for variety can sometimes lead to restlessness, indecisiveness, and a tendency to scatter their energies. Balancing their thirst for new experiences with a focus on completion can be a growth area for Geminis.

Herbal Allies for Gemini

Gemini's herbal allies are those that support the respiratory system, enhance communication, and calm the nervous system, aiding their expressive abilities and grounding their restless energy.

- **Peppermint (Mentha piperita)**: This herb is invigorating and supports clear communication, making it perfect for Gemini. Peppermint also aids digestion and can help alleviate the stress that Geminis might feel due to their active minds.
- **Lavender (Lavandula angustifolia)**: Lavender helps to soothe Gemini's often overactive nervous system, promoting relaxation

and calm. Its gentle fragrance can help ease anxiety and support peaceful sleep.

- **Eucalyptus (Eucalyptus globulus)**: Known for its ability to clear the respiratory system, eucalyptus is beneficial for Geminis, who are ruled by the lungs. It helps enhance breath and voice, which are crucial for effective communication.
- **Lemon Balm (Melissa officinalis)**: This herb is uplifting and can help to calm Gemini's restlessness. Lemon balm enhances mental clarity and focus, aiding Geminis in channeling their intellectual energy productively.

Rituals and Practices

A daily journaling exercise, accompanied by an invigorating herbal tea, offers Gemini an excellent practice to enhance their expressive abilities while grounding their versatile nature.

Journaling Exercise with Herbal Tea for Gemini

1. **Prepare Your Herbal Tea**: Brew a tea blend using Gemini's herbal allies—peppermint for invigoration, lavender for calm, eucalyptus for clear breathing, and lemon balm for focus. This blend supports both the physical act of communication and the mental clarity needed for expression.
2. **Set Your Space**: Choose a quiet and comfortable spot where you can be with your thoughts. Have your journal and a pen ready, along with your cup of herbal tea.
3. **Sip and Reflect**: Begin by sipping your tea, letting its flavors and energies infuse your body and mind. Allow the peppermint to invigorate you, the lavender to calm your thoughts, the eucalyptus to clear your pathways, and the lemon balm to focus your mind.
4. **Journaling Prompts**: Start your journaling with prompts that stimulate your Gemini curiosity and intellect. Explore topics such as 'A new skill I want to learn and why' or 'Different perspectives

on a current issue and my thoughts on them.' Let your thoughts flow freely, exploring each idea that comes to mind.

5. **Reflect and Plan**: After journaling, take a moment to reflect on your writings. Is there a theme that stands out? How can you incorporate these reflections into your daily life or communication with others?

6. **Closing the Practice**: End your session by acknowledging the insights gained and the clarity achieved. Thank the herbal allies for their support in this expressive journey.

This practice not only enhances Gemini's communicative abilities but also serves as a grounding ritual, helping to balance their adaptability with focus. By engaging in this journaling exercise alongside their herbal tea, Geminis can harness their intellectual energy, express their versatile nature, and navigate their world with enhanced clarity and calm.

If you want to see some amazing products, please visit my Virtual Dispensary: https://shift.store/sg1fan23477/retail

Chapter 6: Cancer - The Lunar Healer

Cancer Overview

Cancer, the fourth sign of the zodiac, is deeply influenced by the Moon, reflecting its phases with their emotional ebbs and flows. This water sign is characterized by emotional depth, strong intuition, and a nurturing spirit. Cancers are the caregivers of the zodiac, always ready to offer support and comfort to those they love.

Traits: Cancers possess an unparalleled emotional intelligence, with a profound capacity for empathy and compassion. Their lives are deeply rooted in the home and family, where they create a sanctuary for their loved ones.

Strengths: Among their greatest strengths are their nurturing qualities, loyalty, and ability to connect with others on an emotional level. Cancers are intuitive, often able to sense what others are feeling without words.

Challenges: However, their sensitivity can sometimes lead to moodiness and a tendency to retreat into their shell when hurt. Learning to balance their emotional depth with self-care is crucial for Cancers.

Herbal Allies for Cancer

For the intuitive and emotional Cancer, herbal allies are those that offer comfort, promote emotional balance, and enhance their nurturing qualities.

- **Lemon Balm (Melissa officinalis)**: This herb is known for its soothing properties, reducing stress and anxiety, making it an ideal ally for easing Cancer's emotional turmoil. It also promotes sleep and enhances mood.
- **Chamomile (Matricaria chamomilla)**: Like a warm hug, chamomile comforts and soothes the soul, perfect for the sensitive

Cancer. It aids in relaxation and calms nervous digestive issues, which can arise from emotional stress.

- **Moonflower (Ipomoea alba)**: Aligned with the Moon, moonflower supports Cancer's lunar connections, enhancing intuition and emotional balance. Its blooms opening in the evening remind Cancers to embrace their true nature and beauty, even in darkness.

- **Rose (Rosa spp.)**: Rose aids in healing the heart, promoting self-love and compassion. Its gentle energy supports Cancers in nurturing themselves and others, encouraging an open heart and emotional harmony.

Rituals and Practices

Moonlight infusions are a powerful practice for Cancers, strengthening their connection to the lunar energies and enhancing their intuitive and healing capabilities.

Moonlight Infusion Ritual for Cancer

1. **Prepare Your Infusion**: Choose an herb or a blend of herbs that resonate with Cancer's energy—lemon balm for soothing, chamomile for comfort, moonflower for intuition, and rose for heart healing. Place the herbs in a clear glass jar and cover them with pure water.

2. **Set Your Intention**: As you prepare your infusion, focus on your intention. What emotional healing or intuitive insight do you seek? Hold this intention in your heart as you infuse your herbs with love and care.

3. **Moonlight Charge**: Place your jar outside or on a windowsill under the moonlight. Leave it overnight to absorb the lunar energies. For Cancers, performing this ritual during the Full Moon or New Moon can be especially powerful, aligning with their ruling celestial body's significant phases.

4. **Morning Reflection**: Retrieve your jar at sunrise. As you drink the infusion, reflect on your intention and the healing journey ahead. Visualize the lunar energy within the water nourishing your body, mind, and spirit.

5. **Closing the Practice**: Thank the Moon and your herbal allies for their guidance and support. Carry the sense of calm and clarity with you throughout your day, embracing your natural emotional depth and intuitive powers.

This moonlight infusion ritual allows Cancers to deepen their connection to the lunar energies, embracing their emotional and intuitive strengths. By regularly engaging in this practice, Cancers can enhance their innate healing abilities, offering comfort and nurturing to themselves and those around them.

If you want to see some amazing products, please visit my Virtual Dispensary: https://shift.store/sg1fan23477/retail

Chapter 7: Leo - The Radiant Heart
Leo Overview
Leo, the fifth sign of the zodiac, shines with the brightness of the Sun, its ruling planet. Leos are known for their boldness, creativity, and a heart as warm as the celestial body that guides them. Like the Sun, which is central to our solar system, Leos often find themselves at the center of attention, radiating confidence, generosity, and leadership qualities.

Traits: Leos possess an innate sense of dignity and a desire to be loved and admired. They are creative souls, often drawn to the arts and expressive mediums, where they can showcase their talents and passions.

Strengths: Among their greatest strengths are their courage, loyalty, and big-heartedness. Leos are natural leaders, inspiring others with their optimism and determination. Their warmth and generosity draw people to them, making them excellent friends and allies.

Challenges: However, their need for recognition can sometimes veer into ego-centric behaviors, leading to pridefulness or a tendency to overlook others' contributions. Learning to balance their need for admiration with humility and appreciation for others is a growth area for Leos.

Herbal Allies for Leo
Leo's herbal allies are those that support heart health, encourage open-heartedness, and enhance their natural radiance and leadership abilities.

- **Hawthorn (Crataegus spp.):** This herb is a tonic for the heart, both physically and emotionally. Hawthorn encourages open-heartedness and warmth, supporting Leo's generous nature while protecting their heart.

- **Sunflower (Helianthus annuus)**: Aligned with the Sun, sunflowers embody Leo's radiant spirit. They encourage positivity, strength, and the ability to shine brightly, reflecting Leo's natural leadership qualities.
- **Rosemary (Rosmarinus officinalis)**: This herb supports Leo's mental clarity and creativity. Rosemary aids in enhancing memory and concentration, vital for Leos to manifest their creative visions.
- **Goldenseal (Hydrastis canadensis)**: While not directly a heart herb, goldenseal is included for its association with the Sun and its ability to purify and protect. It supports Leo's vibrant health, allowing their natural radiance to shine through.

Rituals and Practices

Self-love rituals are essential for Leos, encouraging their natural radiance, nurturing their leadership qualities, and balancing their vibrant energy with humility.

Self-Love Ritual for Leo

1. **Prepare Your Space**: Create a warm, inviting environment that reflects Leo's sunny disposition. Use gold, yellow, and orange colors in your decor, and consider placing sunflowers or images of the Sun around you.
2. **Select Your Herbs**: Craft a heart-warming tea blend with hawthorn for heart health, rosemary for clarity, and a touch of goldenseal for its purifying qualities. As you prepare your tea, focus on your intentions for self-love and radiance.
3. **Set Your Intentions**: As you sip your tea, reflect on your strengths and areas for growth. Acknowledge your need for recognition and ponder how you can fulfill this need through self-appreciation and acknowledging others' contributions.

4. **Journaling Exercise**: Write down what makes you unique and worthy of love—not just from others but from yourself. Include your talents, generosity, and how you uplift those around you.

5. **Affirmation**: Close your ritual with affirmations that reinforce self-love and humility. Repeat affirmations such as "I radiate love and warmth," "I acknowledge and appreciate the light in others," and "I lead with my heart, shining brightly for all to see."

6. **Closing the Practice**: Thank yourself for taking the time to nurture your heart and spirit. Carry the warmth and love from your ritual into the world, sharing your light in a way that uplifts and inspires those around you.

This self-love ritual for Leo fosters an environment where Leos can shine their brightest while staying grounded in the humility and warmth of their radiant hearts. Through regular practice, Leos can balance their natural leadership and creativity with a generous and open heart, truly embodying the radiant spirit of their sign.

If you want to see some amazing products, please visit my Virtual Dispensary: https://shift.store/sg1fan23477/retail

Chapter 8: Virgo - The Earthly Alchemist

Virgo Overview

Virgo, the sixth sign of the zodiac, embodies the essence of meticulous analysis, practicality, and a relentless pursuit of perfection. Ruled by Mercury, the planet of communication and intellect, Virgos are the problem solvers of the zodiac, applying their sharp analytical skills to serve others and improve the world around them.

Traits: Virgos are known for their detail-oriented nature, often able to see and solve problems long before they become apparent to others. Their earth sign nature grounds them in practicality, ensuring their solutions are not just theoretical but applicable.

Strengths: Among their greatest strengths are their reliability, meticulousness, and a profound sense of duty. Virgos excel in situations where precision and attention to detail are required, making them invaluable in any team or project.

Challenges: However, their quest for perfection can sometimes become a double-edged sword, leading to excessive criticism of themselves and others, or paralysis by analysis. Learning to balance their high standards with acceptance of imperfection is a crucial lesson for Virgos.

Herbal Allies for Virgo

For the methodical and health-conscious Virgo, herbal allies are those that support digestion (reflecting their analytical nature), ease worry, and promote grounding.

- **Ginger (Zingiber officinale)**: This root supports Virgo's digestive system, offering relief from stress-induced stomach issues. It also serves as a warming, energizing herb that can invigorate Virgo's sometimes overworked system.
- **Peppermint (Mentha piperita)**: Peppermint aids digestion and soothes nervous stomachs, common ailments for hardworking

Virgos. Its refreshing nature also helps clear the mind, enhancing focus and concentration.

- **Chamomile (Matricaria chamomilla)**: Known for its calming properties, chamomile helps ease Virgo's worries and soothes their perfectionist tendencies, promoting relaxation and a peaceful state of mind.
- **Dandelion (Taraxacum officinale)**: This herb is a grounding force for Virgo, helping to detoxify and rebalance an overtaxed system. It supports liver health, a crucial aspect for those who internalize stress and anxiety.

Rituals and Practices

Organizational and cleansing rituals play a significant role in decluttering both the physical and mental spaces of Virgo, promoting a sense of purity and efficiency.

Organizational Ritual for Virgo

1. **Prepare Your Space**: Start with a clean and uncluttered space. Virgos thrive in environments where order and efficiency reign, so consider this your foundation.
2. **Select Your Herbs**: Brew a tea blend using Virgo's herbal allies—ginger for digestive health, peppermint for focus, chamomile for calming, and dandelion for grounding and detoxification.
3. **Set Your Intentions**: As you sip your tea, set intentions for the organizational tasks ahead. Focus on what you wish to achieve, whether it's decluttering your workspace, organizing your thoughts, or planning your week.
4. **Cleansing and Organizing**: Begin your organizing ritual. Start small, focusing on one area at a time. As you organize, visualize yourself clearing away mental clutter and worry, creating space for clarity and efficiency.
5. **Meditation Break**: Midway, take a short break to meditate, focusing on your breath and the feeling of release that comes with

letting go of what no longer serves you. This can help recenter your focus and renew your energy.

6. **Gratitude and Reflection**: Once completed, reflect on the work done and express gratitude for the space and clarity you've created. Acknowledge the importance of this external order in supporting your internal well-being.

7. **Closing the Practice**: End your ritual with a commitment to maintain this order, recognizing it as an ongoing process that supports your mental and physical health.

This organizational ritual for Virgo is a powerful tool for maintaining efficiency and clarity, both in their physical surroundings and their mental space. By regularly engaging in this practice, Virgos can balance their analytical and practical nature with a nurturing approach to self-care, promoting a healthy, balanced lifestyle.

If you want to see some amazing products, please visit my Virtual Dispensary: https://shift.store/sg1fan23477/retail

Chapter 9: Libra - The Harmonious Balance
Libra Overview

Libra, the seventh sign of the zodiac, is the epitome of balance, harmony, and fairness. Ruled by Venus, the planet of love and beauty, Libras are drawn to all things aesthetic and seek equilibrium in every aspect of life. They are the diplomats of the zodiac, using their innate sense of justice to mediate conflicts and create peace.

Traits: Libras are characterized by their sociability, charm, and a strong sense of right and wrong. Their ability to see multiple sides of an argument makes them excellent mediators, though this same trait can lead to indecision.

Strengths: Among their greatest strengths are their diplomacy, artistic eye, and unwavering commitment to fairness. Libras have a unique ability to create harmony in chaotic situations, making them valuable friends and partners.

Challenges: However, their desire for balance can sometimes manifest as indecision, as Libras may find it challenging to choose between options. Additionally, their focus on harmony might lead them to avoid necessary confrontations, affecting personal growth and relationships.

Herbal Allies for Libra

For the aesthetically inclined and harmony-seeking Libra, herbal allies are those that promote balance, especially in the kidneys (associated with Libra in traditional astrology), and support overall well-being.

- **Kidney Vetch (Anthyllis vulneraria)**: This herb is traditionally used to support kidney health, aligning with Libra's association with this organ. It helps in maintaining the body's balance of fluids and electrolytes, mirroring Libra's quest for equilibrium.
- **Rose (Rosa spp.)**: As a symbol of Venus, rose supports Libra's ruling planet, enhancing beauty and love in their surroundings. It also helps in balancing the emotional heart, encouraging self-love and understanding.

- **Jasmine (Jasminum officinale)**: Jasmine's sweet aroma is uplifting and helps to balance mood swings, a boon for Libras seeking emotional stability. It's also known for its love-enhancing properties, resonating with Libra's Venusian influence.
- **Lemon Balm (Melissa officinalis)**: Lemon balm promotes mental balance, reducing anxiety and stress. Its calming properties can help Libras find clarity in decision-making, easing their characteristic indecisiveness.

Rituals and Practices

Balancing tea ceremonies provide a moment of reflection and equilibrium in Libra's life, encouraging inner peace and decision-making clarity.

Balancing Tea Ceremony for Libra

1. **Prepare Your Space**: Create a harmonious setting that reflects Libra's love for beauty. Use aesthetic elements like flowers, art, and soft music to enhance the atmosphere.
2. **Select Your Herbs**: Craft a tea blend using Libra's herbal allies—kidney vetch for physical balance, rose for emotional harmony, jasmine for mood balancing, and lemon balm for mental clarity.
3. **Set Your Intention**: As you prepare your tea, focus on your intention for balance in all aspects of your life. Consider the areas where you seek equilibrium, whether in relationships, work, or personal growth.
4. **Perform the Ceremony**: Slowly pour hot water over your tea blend, watching as the herbs release their essence. As you do so, visualize the balance you seek infusing into the water, ready to sip and absorb.
5. **Meditation and Reflection**: While sipping your tea, meditate on the qualities of balance and harmony. Reflect on decisions you need to make, viewing them from a place of inner calm and balance.

6. **Journaling**: After meditation, write down insights or decisions that arose during your reflection. Note any steps you can take to bring more balance into your life.

7. **Closing the Practice**: Express gratitude for the insights gained and the peace experienced. Commit to carrying the harmony from your tea ceremony into your daily life, making decisions from a place of balanced clarity.

This balancing tea ceremony for Libra is a nurturing ritual that aligns with their quest for harmony and beauty. By incorporating it into their routine, Libras can enhance their natural diplomacy, make more decisive choices, and cultivate a deeper sense of peace and equilibrium in their lives.

If you want to see some amazing products, please visit my Virtual Dispensary: https://shift.store/sg1fan23477/retail

Chapter 10: Scorpio - The Mystical Transformer
Scorpio Overview

Scorpio, the eighth sign of the zodiac, is a wellspring of power, depth, and mystery. Governed by Pluto, the planet of transformation and regeneration, Scorpios are known for their intense emotional depth, capacity for profound change, and innate understanding of life's more hidden aspects. They navigate the world with a keen perception, unearthing truths that lie beneath the surface.

Traits: Scorpios are characterized by their determination, loyalty, and a compelling aura of mystique. Their presence is often felt before it is seen, wielding an energy that is both intriguing and formidable.

Strengths: Among their greatest strengths are resilience, strategic skills, and a powerful intuition. Scorpios possess a unique ability to transform themselves and their surroundings, thriving in situations that demand change and depth.

Challenges: However, their strength can also be their vulnerability. The intensity of their emotions can lead to secrecy and a fear of vulnerability. Scorpios might struggle with letting go of control and trusting others, their protective instincts sometimes perceived as manipulation.

Herbal Allies for Scorpio

For the transformative and deeply introspective Scorpio, herbal allies are those that support detoxification, emotional release, and spiritual awakening.

- **Bloodroot (Sanguinaria canadensis):** This powerful herb is known for its deep cleansing properties, mirroring Scorpio's transformative processes. It must be used with knowledge and respect, as it reflects Scorpio's potent nature.
- **Blackthorn (Prunus spinosa):** Blackthorn's ability to thrive in harsh conditions resonates with Scorpio's resilience. It symbolizes the process of overcoming emotional barriers, aiding in healing and protection.
- **Garlic (Allium sativum):** A natural purifier, garlic supports Scorpio's need for detoxification and protection from negativity. It strengthens the immune system, mirroring Scorpio's ability to regenerate and heal.
- **Yarrow (Achillea millefolium):** Yarrow is known for its ability to heal physical and emotional wounds, resonating with Scorpio's transformative healing processes. It aids in psychic protection and opens the path to spiritual insight.

Rituals and Practices

Intense meditation practices can help Scorpio delve into their depths, unlocking mysteries within and fostering a transformative spiritual journey.

Intense Meditation Practice for Scorpio

1. **Prepare Your Space:** Choose a secluded, quiet space where you won't be disturbed. Scorpio's meditation practice benefits from solitude, enhancing the depth of the experience.
2. **Select Your Herbs:** Create a blend of Scorpio's herbal allies. You can use them in a diffuser, as incense, or in a sachet to have close by during meditation. Their energies will support your journey inward.
3. **Set Your Intention:** As you begin, set an intention for your meditation. Whether it's to uncover hidden aspects of yourself,

release emotional blockages, or seek guidance on your transformative journey, hold this intention in your heart.

4. **Deep Dive Meditation**: Start with deep, grounding breaths, then allow your consciousness to dive deep into the core of your being. Visualize yourself descending into the depths of a dark, still pool. With each breath, go deeper, exploring the hidden, shadowy aspects of your psyche.

5. **Confront and Release**: In this deep state, confront the emotions or memories that arise. Scorpio's practice is not about surface-level peace but about confronting and transforming the deep-seated. Use visualization to release these energies, seeing them dissolve into light or be washed away by cleansing waters.

6. **Rising Renewed**: Begin to ascend from the depths, visualizing yourself emerging transformed and renewed. With each layer you pass through, feel lighter, more purified, and empowered.

7. **Reflection and Journaling**: After the meditation, take time to journal your experiences, insights, or any emotions that arose. This practice helps to integrate your transformative journey into your conscious awareness.

8. **Closing the Practice**: Thank yourself and the universe for the deep work done. Carry the insights and transformations with you, allowing them to guide your actions and interactions.

This intense meditation practice for Scorpio supports their natural inclination towards transformation, depth, and regeneration. By regularly engaging in this practice, Scorpios can harness their powerful emotional and spiritual energies, leading to profound personal growth and awakening.

If you want to see some amazing products, please visit my Virtual Dispensary: https://shift.store/sg1fan23477/retail

Chapter 11: Sagittarius - The Philosophical Explorer

Sagittarius Overview

Sagittarius, the ninth sign of the zodiac, is a beacon of freedom, optimism, and a thirst for knowledge. Ruled by Jupiter, the planet of expansion and abundance, Sagittarians are characterized by their love for adventure, philosophical pursuits, and the endless search for truth and wisdom. They approach life with an open heart and an open mind, always aiming to broaden their horizons.

Traits: Sagittarians are known for their vibrant energy, infectious enthusiasm, and a profound sense of independence. They possess an innate need to explore, whether it's through physical travel, intellectual pursuits, or spiritual exploration.

Strengths: Among their greatest strengths are their optimistic outlook, adaptability, and fearless spirit. Sagittarians inspire others with their love for life and relentless pursuit of growth and experience.

Challenges: However, their love for freedom can sometimes manifest as restlessness or a reluctance to commit, whether to people or situations. Learning to balance their need for adventure with moments of stillness and reflection is a crucial lesson for Sagittarians.

Herbal Allies for Sagittarius

For the adventurous and freedom-loving Sagittarius, herbal allies are those that support liver function (reflecting their ruling planet Jupiter's association with this organ), cleanse the blood, and sustain their energetic spirit.

- **Dandelion (Taraxacum officinale)**: This herb is a powerful liver cleanser, supporting detoxification and overall vitality. It embodies Sagittarius' resilient and adventurous spirit, thriving in diverse environments.
- **Milk Thistle (Silybum marianum)**: Milk thistle is known for its protective and regenerative effects on the liver, helping to maintain the health and vitality crucial for Sagittarius' explorations.

- **Turmeric (Curcuma longa)**: With its anti-inflammatory properties, turmeric supports Sagittarius' active lifestyle, helping to maintain joint health and overall well-being during their adventures.
- **Ginger (Zingiber officinale)**: Ginger energizes and stimulates, mirroring Sagittarius' zest for life. It also aids digestion, which can be beneficial during travel and exploration of new cuisines.

Rituals and Practices

Travel rituals can provide protection, energy, and a sense of grounding for Sagittarius during their explorations, ensuring their adventures are both enriching and safe.

Travel Ritual for Sagittarius

1. **Prepare Your Herbal Allies**: Before embarking on your journey, prepare a blend of Sagittarius' herbal allies. Create a tea mixture or an herbal sachet with dandelion, milk thistle, turmeric, and ginger to carry with you.
2. **Set Your Intention**: Sit quietly and focus on your upcoming journey. What do you wish to learn, experience, or discover? Set an intention that resonates with your Sagittarian spirit of exploration.
3. **Energize Your Allies**: Hold your herbal blend in your hands, visualizing it being infused with the energy of protection, health, and curiosity. Imagine this energy safeguarding you throughout your travels.
4. **Blessing for the Journey**: Speak a blessing or a short prayer over your herbal blend, asking for safe travels, enriching experiences, and personal growth. Acknowledge the interconnectedness of all beings and express gratitude for the opportunity to explore.
5. **Carry With You**: Keep your herbal blend close throughout your journey. Whether as a tea to sip or a sachet to smell, let it be a

constant reminder of your intention and a source of protection and vitality.

6. **Journaling**: Keep a travel journal, documenting your experiences, thoughts, and the wisdom gained along the way. Reflect on how each experience relates to your initial intention and what it teaches you about yourself and the world.

7. **Gratitude Ritual**: Upon your return, perform a simple ritual of gratitude. Acknowledge the lessons learned, the experiences had, and the growth achieved. Offer thanks to your herbal allies for their protection and support.

This travel ritual for Sagittarius reinforces the sign's innate desire for adventure and exploration while providing a spiritual framework that grounds their experiences in personal growth and wisdom. By incorporating these practices, Sagittarians can fully embrace their philosophical explorer archetype, journeying with purpose, protection, and an open heart.

If you want to see some amazing products, please visit my Virtual Dispensary: https://shift.store/sg1fan23477/retail

Chapter 12: Capricorn - The Structured Sage

Capricorn Overview

Capricorn, the tenth sign of the zodiac, embodies the pinnacle of ambition, discipline, and practicality. Ruled by Saturn, the planet of structure and responsibility, Capricorns are the architects of the zodiac, building their lives and careers with meticulous planning and steadfast determination. Their methodical approach to life ensures they are often seen as the pillars within their communities, offering strength and stability to those around them.

Traits: Capricorns are characterized by their strong work ethic, patience, and unwavering focus. They possess a natural leadership ability, often taking charge in professional settings and personal endeavors alike.

Strengths: Among their greatest strengths are their resilience, reliability, and unmatched discipline. Capricorns have the unique ability to set long-term goals and pursue them with relentless dedication, making them successful in virtually any endeavor they undertake.

Challenges: However, their strength can sometimes morph into rigidity, making it difficult for Capricorns to adapt to change or embrace spontaneity. Their focus on achievement can also lead to a neglect of emotional needs, both their own and those of others.

Herbal Allies for Capricorn

For the ambitious and disciplined Capricorn, herbal allies are those that support bone health, reflecting their symbolic skeletal association, and offer grounding to balance their structured nature.

- **Horsetail (Equisetum arvense)**: Rich in silica, horsetail is beneficial for bone health and connective tissues, supporting Capricorn's skeletal association. It symbolizes the strength and steadfastness of Capricorn.

- **Comfrey (Symphytum officinale)**: Known for its healing properties, particularly in relation to bones and skin, comfrey aligns with Capricorn's need for physical support due to their hardworking nature.
- **Nettle (Urtica dioica)**: Nettle is rich in minerals crucial for bone health and vitality, supporting Capricorn's enduring energy. It also offers a grounding energy, balancing Capricorn's ambitious drive.
- **Alfalfa (Medicago sativa)**: Alfalfa is deeply nourishing and supports overall vitality and bone health. It encourages flexibility and adaptability, qualities that Capricorns benefit from integrating into their disciplined lives.

Rituals and Practices

Grounding exercises are essential for Capricorn, helping them maintain a balance between their structured approach to life and the need for flexibility and emotional nourishment.

Grounding Exercise for Capricorn

1. **Prepare Your Space**: Choose a quiet, comfortable area where you can be undisturbed. Natural settings are particularly beneficial for Capricorns to feel connected to the earth.
2. **Select Your Herbs**: Prepare a tea blend with Capricorn's herbal allies—horsetail for strength, comfrey for healing, nettle for vitality, and alfalfa for nourishment. Sip this tea to begin the grounding process, inviting flexibility and resilience into your body and mind.
3. **Set Your Intention**: As you drink your tea, set an intention for balance and grounding. Acknowledge your achievements while inviting in the wisdom of adaptability and the richness of emotional experience.
4. **Grounding Visualization**: Sit or stand comfortably, imagining roots extending from the soles of your feet deep into the earth.

Feel the stability and nourishment coming from this connection, supporting your ambitions while reminding you of the importance of flexibility and growth.

5. **Breath Work**: Incorporate deep, mindful breathing to help release rigidity in both body and mind. With each exhale, imagine letting go of stress, tension, and the need for control. With each inhale, draw in flexibility, openness, and peace.

6. **Reflection and Journaling**: After your grounding exercise, take a moment to journal about your experiences. Reflect on the balance between your structured approach to life and areas where you can invite more spontaneity and emotional expression.

7. **Closing the Practice**: Express gratitude for the strength and stability you possess, as well as for the new insights into flexibility and emotional openness. Commit to incorporating these grounding practices into your routine, recognizing them as vital components of your success and well-being.

This grounding exercise for Capricorn supports their need for structure and ambition while encouraging the incorporation of flexibility and emotional openness into their lives. By regularly engaging in this practice, Capricorns can maintain their characteristic determination and reliability, balanced with a newfound adaptability and a deeper connection to their emotional landscape.

If you want to see some amazing products, please visit my Virtual Dispensary: https://shift.store/sg1fan23477/retail

Chapter 13: Aquarius - The Visionary Rebel
Aquarius Overview

Aquarius, the eleventh sign of the zodiac, is the embodiment of innovation, intellect, and idealism. Governed by Uranus, the planet of sudden change and enlightenment, Aquarians are forward-thinking visionaries, often ahead of their time. They possess a unique blend of social consciousness and individuality, striving to make the world a better place through radical ideas and communal efforts.

Traits: Aquarians are known for their independence, creativity, and a deep sense of humanitarianism. They approach life with a unique perspective, valuing freedom of expression and thought.

Strengths: Among their greatest strengths are their inventiveness, ability to think outside the box, and dedication to community and social causes. Aquarians inspire change and progress, challenging the status quo with their visionary outlook.

Challenges: However, their strength in detachment and focus on the collective can sometimes lead to a sense of aloofness or difficulty in forming deep personal connections. Balancing their visionary ideals with emotional presence is a growth area for Aquarians.

Herbal Allies for Aquarius

For the intellectually stimulated and socially oriented Aquarius, herbal allies are those that support the nervous system, calm the mind, and encourage emotional connection.

- **Skullcap (Scutellaria lateriflora)**: This herb is known for its calming effects on the nervous system, helping to ease the mental buzz that Aquarians often experience due to their constant flow of ideas and plans.

- **Lemon Balm (Melissa officinalis)**: Lemon balm offers a soothing effect, reducing stress and anxiety. It supports Aquarians in finding calm and focus amidst their revolutionary pursuits.
- **Passionflower (Passiflora incarnata)**: Passionflower is beneficial for promoting relaxation and deep sleep, assisting Aquarians in disconnecting from their mental activity and nurturing their emotional well-being.
- **Gotu Kola (Centella asiatica)**: Gotu kola supports mental clarity and enhances meditation, aligning with Aquarius' need for innovation while grounding their thoughts in practicality.

Rituals and Practices

Community herbal gatherings provide a perfect outlet for Aquarians to engage with their love for social involvement, innovation, and shared learning.

Community Herbal Gathering for Aquarius

1. **Gathering Theme**: Decide on a theme that resonates with the Aquarian spirit of innovation and community service. It could range from creating herbal remedies for local shelters, to workshops on sustainable living, or discussions on the intersection of technology and natural healing.
2. **Invite Like-Minded Individuals**: Aquarians thrive in the company of fellow visionaries and rebels. Use social media or community boards to invite individuals who share your interest in herbalism and social change.
3. **Prepare Your Space**: Choose a space that encourages open communication and interaction. Arrange seating in circles or semi-circles to facilitate discussion and collaboration.
4. **Select Your Herbs**: Highlight Aquarius' herbal allies in your gathering. Prepare teas or tinctures with skullcap, lemon balm, passionflower, and gotu kola to share with attendees, explaining their significance and benefits.

5. **Incorporate Technology**: As the sign most associated with technological advancement, consider incorporating technology into your gathering. This could be through virtual reality experiences of herbal gardens, apps for identifying plants, or online platforms for sharing recipes and ideas.

6. **Facilitate Open Discussion**: Encourage attendees to share their knowledge, ideas, and experiences with herbalism. Facilitate a brainstorming session on innovative ways to use herbs for community benefit.

7. **Actionable Outcomes**: Conclude the gathering with a focus on actionable outcomes, whether it's a community garden project, a collective blog on herbal remedies, or a plan to distribute homemade herbal products to those in need.

8. **Closing Ritual**: End the gathering with a group meditation or a collective intention-setting exercise, focusing on the positive impact your community can make through the power of herbalism and shared vision.

This community herbal gathering for Aquarius feeds their need for social involvement and innovation, providing a platform for Aquarians to channel their visionary ideas into tangible community benefits. Through these gatherings, Aquarians can find a balance between their intellectual pursuits and the emotional richness of community connection, fostering a sense of belonging and purpose in their quest for progress and change.

If you want to see some amazing products, please visit my Virtual Dispensary: https://shift.store/sg1fan23477/retail

Chapter 14: Pisces - The Dreamy Empath
Pisces Overview

In the celestial tapestry of the zodiac, Pisces emerges as the final constellation, embodying the essence of compassion, boundless creativity, and an ethereal connection to the unseen realms. Governed by Neptune, the planet that dissolves boundaries and fosters dreams, Pisceans are the mystics and poets of the zodiac, navigating the world with an open heart and an intuitive spirit.

Traits: Pisceans are fluid and adaptable, much like the water they symbolize. They possess an uncanny ability to feel deeply, often absorbing the emotions of those around them like a psychic sponge. This makes them incredibly empathetic, but it can also lead to a sense of overwhelm and a desire for escape into their rich inner world or through creative expression.

Strengths: The strengths of Pisces lie in their vast imaginative powers, their artistic talents, and their limitless capacity for empathy. They have a natural inclination towards healing and service, often finding fulfillment in helping others or in creating beauty that touches the soul.

Challenges: Yet, the depth of their emotional world can sometimes lead Pisces to seek refuge in escapism, whether through daydreams, art, or less wholesome means. Finding a balance between their ethereal nature and the demands of the tangible world is a constant dance for those born under this sign.

Herbal Allies for Pisces

To support the dreamy and empathetic nature of Pisces, certain herbs stand out as allies, offering grounding, enhancing their natural intuition, and fostering a connection to the dream world.

- **Mugwort (Artemisia vulgaris)**: This powerful herb acts as a bridge to the subconscious, enhancing dream recall and lucidity.

For Pisces, mugwort can deepen their exploration of the dream world, offering insights and creative inspiration.

- **Lavender (Lavandula angustifolia)**: With its soothing aroma, lavender is a balm for the often-overwhelmed Piscean soul, promoting calm, reducing anxiety, and facilitating a peaceful state of mind conducive to insightful dreaming.
- **Chamomile (Matricaria chamomilla)**: This gentle herb offers comfort and relaxation, easing the emotional and psychic sensitivity that Pisces often experiences, and helping them find a serene space for restful sleep and dreams.
- **Lemon Balm (Melissa officinalis)**: Known for its ability to lift spirits and alleviate melancholy, lemon balm supports Pisces' emotional wellbeing, clearing the mind for positive and healing dream experiences.

Rituals and Practices

To navigate their rich inner world and channel their creativity, Pisces can engage in dreamwork rituals, which not only enhance their nocturnal journeys but also offer insights into their waking life and creative endeavors.

Dreamwork Ritual for Pisces

1. **Preparation**: Begin by creating a serene environment conducive to relaxation and introspection. Incorporate elements like soft lighting, comfortable bedding, and perhaps a notebook and pen for journaling.
2. **Herbal Tea Ceremony**: Brew a tea with a blend of Pisces' herbal allies, focusing on your intention to explore the depths of your dreams. As you sip the tea, allow its calming energy to wash over you, setting the stage for profound dream experiences.
3. **Journaling Intentions**: Before settling into bed, write down any specific questions or themes you wish to explore in your dreams.

This act of intention-setting can help guide your subconscious explorations.

4. **Guided Meditation**: Engage in a brief meditation or visualization, imagining yourself descending into a peaceful, luminous dreamscape where clarity and insight await. Envision a safe, sacred space where you can receive messages from your subconscious.

5. **Sleep Ritual**: As you lie down to sleep, repeat a mantra or affirmation that reinforces your intention to remember and learn from your dreams, such as "I open myself to the wisdom of my dreams."

6. **Morning Reflection**: Upon waking, immediately record any dreams or impressions in your journal, even if they seem inconsequential. Reflect on the symbols, emotions, and narratives of your dreams, exploring their relevance to your waking life or creative projects.

7. **Integration Practice**: Consider ways to integrate the insights gained from your dreams into your daily life. This might involve creative expression, such as painting or writing, or practical actions inspired by your dream revelations.

8. **Gratitude**: Close your dreamwork practice with a moment of gratitude for the insights received and the creativity inspired by your dreams. Acknowledge the unique gift of your Piscean sensitivity and imagination.

By regularly engaging in these dreamwork rituals, Pisces can harness their profound empathy and creativity, turning their dreams into wellsprings of inspiration and insight. This practice allows Pisces to navigate their inner seas with confidence, bringing the treasures of the deep to the shores of their everyday lives.

If you want to see some amazing products, please visit my Virtual Dispensary: https://shift.store/sg1fan23477/retail

Chapter 15: Creating Your Personal Zodiac Garden

Embarking on the creation of a zodiac garden is a magical way to deepen your connection with the celestial energies that guide the natural world. This sacred space serves not only as a sanctuary of beauty and tranquility but also as a living embodiment of the astrological influences that resonate with your personal journey. Herein, we delve into the art and science of designing a garden infused with zodiacal essence, tending to it with the cycles of the heavens in mind, and honoring the astrological seasons through ritual and celebration.

Garden Planning: Reflecting Astrological Energies

Designing a zodiac garden requires a blend of creativity, intuition, and an understanding of astrological principles. Begin by mapping out your garden space, considering the cardinal directions and the elements associated with them—Fire (South), Earth (North), Air (East), and Water (West). Each section can be dedicated to the zodiac signs of the corresponding element, creating a harmonious balance of energies.

- **Sign-Specific Sections**: Allocate areas of your garden to each zodiac sign, choosing plants that resonate with the energies of that sign. For example, fiery Aries might feature bold red flowers and pioneering species, while watery Pisces could include lush ferns and water features that reflect its fluid, mystical nature.
- **Pathways and Sacred Spaces**: Incorporate winding pathways that invite exploration, leading to secluded spots for meditation

and reflection. These can be aligned with the natural energy flow of the garden, creating a journey through the astrological year.

- **Symbolic Decorations**: Adorn your garden with symbols and artifacts that reflect the qualities of each sign, such as sculptures, stones, or colored accents. Consider integrating a central feature that represents the Sun, the giver of life and the celestial body that governs the zodiac.

Plant Care: Astrologically Significant Practices

Tending to your zodiac garden offers a unique opportunity to engage in practices that honor the astrological significance of each plant and the lunar and planetary cycles.

- **Planting by the Moon**: Align your planting, pruning, and harvesting activities with the phases of the Moon. The waxing phase, from new to full moon, is ideal for planting and transplanting, encouraging growth. The waning phase, from full to new moon, is better for pruning, weeding, and harvesting, focusing energy on root development.

- **Planetary Hours**: Each day is governed by a specific planet, influencing various activities and energies. Consider carrying out garden tasks in harmony with the planetary hours that correspond to the plants you are tending to, enhancing their growth and vitality.

- **Astrological Correspondences**: Use the astrological correspondences of plants to inform your care practices. For example, Mars-ruled plants may thrive with more direct action and pruning, while Venus-ruled plants might benefit from gentler care and attention to aesthetics.

Seasonal Rituals: Celebrating Astrological Seasons

Your zodiac garden is not only a place of cultivation but also a sacred space for celebrating the turning of the astrological wheel through the seasons.

- **Solstices and Equinoxes**: Mark the cardinal points of the astrological year—the solstices and equinoxes—with special rituals or gatherings. These can include planting new seeds at the Spring Equinox, celebrating abundance at the Summer Solstice, harvesting at the Autumn Equinox, and reflecting and releasing at the Winter Solstice.

- **Zodiac Sign Celebrations**: Honor the entry of the Sun into a new zodiac sign with a ritual that celebrates the qualities of that sign. This could involve focusing on the plants associated with that sign, meditating on the sign's themes, or creating art that reflects its energies.

- **Moon Gardens**: For those drawn to the mysteries of the night, consider dedicating a section of your garden to moon-loving plants, such as white flowers and night-blooming species. Celebrate full moons with gatherings that involve moon gazing, drum circles, or simply quiet reflection in the moonlit beauty of your garden.

Creating your personal zodiac garden is a journey of connecting with the cosmos, the earth, and your inner self. Through thoughtful planning, attuned care practices, and seasonal celebrations, your garden becomes a living tapestry of astrological wisdom—a sanctuary where the stars descend to whisper secrets to those willing to listen.

If you want to see some amazing products, please visit my Virtual Dispensary: https://shift.store/sg1fan23477/retail

Chapter 16: The Zodiac Kitchen - Cooking with the Stars

Embarking on a culinary journey through the zodiac brings a magical fusion of flavors and energies into your kitchen. Cooking with the stars involves more than just preparing meals; it's about infusing your dishes with the celestial essence of each zodiac sign, transforming the act of cooking into a sacred ritual that honors the unique qualities and elements of the astrological wheel. This chapter explores astrological cooking techniques, recipes tailored to enhance the energies of each sign, and the art of celebrating the zodiac seasons through seasonal feasts that resonate with the cosmic rhythm.

Astrological Cooking: Recipes and Kitchen Rituals

Astrological cooking requires an intuitive blend of ingredients, intentions, and timing, with each zodiac sign inspiring unique recipes that embody its spirit. By incorporating herbs, spices, and foods associated with each sign, you can create dishes that enhance specific energies, support wellbeing, and bring balance to the body and soul.

- **Aries:** Bold flavors and spicy dishes ignite Aries' fiery nature. Think peppery salads, spicy soups, and dishes that use ingredients like mustard, horseradish, and chili. Cooking rituals can involve setting bold intentions and infusing your dishes with courage and initiative.

- **Taurus:** Comforting, earthy meals that indulge the senses are ideal for Taurus. Rich stews, decadent desserts, and hearty bread embody this sign's love for luxurious flavors. Taurus cooking rituals focus on gratitude, savoring each flavor and texture as a celebration of the earth's bounty.

- **Gemini:** Light, versatile dishes that encourage sharing and conversation suit Gemini's airy nature. Think tapas, finger foods, and vibrant salads. Gemini-inspired kitchen rituals involve playful experimentation with flavors and creating meals that spark curiosity and connection.

- **Cancer**: Nourishing, home-cooked meals that evoke a sense of comfort and care reflect Cancer's nurturing spirit. Soups, casseroles, and family recipes passed down through generations are perfect. Cooking rituals for Cancer focus on infusing dishes with love and protective energy.
- **Leo**: Creative, colorful dishes that command attention and spark joy resonate with Leo's fiery and expressive energy. Grilled meats, dramatic desserts, and meals with a touch of gold or saffron fit this sign's regal tastes. Leo kitchen rituals emphasize cooking with passion and pride, celebrating the joy of creation.
- **Virgo**: Health-conscious, meticulously prepared dishes that utilize fresh, organic ingredients align with Virgo's earthy and detail-oriented nature. Salads, whole grains, and detoxifying teas are ideal. Virgo cooking rituals focus on the intention of healing and purification, blessing each meal with wishes for wellness.
- **Libra**: Elegant, balanced dishes that please both the palate and the eye suit Libra's love for harmony and beauty. Delicate pastries, balanced entrées with a perfect mix of flavors, and artfully presented plates. Libra kitchen rituals involve creating beauty and balance, setting intentions for peace and partnership.
- **Scorpio**: Intense, rich flavors and dishes that invoke mystery and transformation capture Scorpio's watery depth. Meals with ingredients like pomegranate, dark chocolate, and deep red wines. Scorpio cooking rituals delve into the transformative power of food, cooking as an act of deep, personal alchemy.
- **Sagittarius**: Exotic, adventurous dishes that reflect a fusion of cultures ignite Sagittarius' fiery and exploratory spirit. International cuisines, spicy curries, and dishes with bold, unexpected flavor combinations. Sagittarius kitchen rituals focus on the joy of discovery and the celebration of diversity.

- **Capricorn**: Traditional, time-honored recipes that embody the essence of craftsmanship and discipline resonate with Capricorn's earthy solidity. Roasts, artisanal cheeses, and dishes prepared with classic techniques. Capricorn cooking rituals emphasize respect for tradition and the dedication to craft.
- **Aquarius**: Innovative, unconventional dishes that challenge the norm suit Aquarius' airy and avant-garde nature. Molecular gastronomy, plant-based innovations, and meals that incorporate cutting-edge culinary techniques. Aquarius kitchen rituals involve setting intentions for innovation and social change.
- **Pisces**: Fluid, imaginative dishes that evoke a sense of the ethereal and mystical align with Pisces' watery, dreamy essence. Seafood, soups with subtle flavors, and dishes that incorporate alcohol like wine or spirits. Pisces cooking rituals focus on connecting with the spiritual and emotional resonance of food, cooking as a form of meditation and creativity.

Seasonal Feasts: Celebrating the Zodiac Seasons

Celebrating the zodiac seasons through culinary feasts involves crafting menus that resonate with the energy of the Sun's transit through each sign. This is a time to honor the qualities of each zodiac sign, gathering friends and family for meals that reflect the current astrological season.

- **Spring (Aries, Taurus, Gemini)**: Celebrate rebirth and awakening with vibrant, fresh dishes. Think spring greens, dairy products for Taurus, and light, airy desserts for Gemini.
- **Summer (Cancer, Leo, Virgo)**: Focus on warmth and abundance with comforting, heartwarming meals for Cancer, bold and dramatic dishes for Leo, and health-conscious, meticulous preparations for Virgo.
- **Autumn (Libra, Scorpio, Sagittarius)**: Embrace balance, transformation, and exploration with beautifully balanced plates for

Libra, deep, intense flavors for Scorpio, and adventurous, exotic cuisines for Sagittarius.

- **Winter (Capricorn, Aquarius, Pisces):** Reflect tradition, innovation, and mysticism with hearty, traditional meals for Capricorn, futuristic and unconventional dishes for Aquarius, and soulful, comforting foods for Pisces.

By aligning your culinary practices with the stars, you not only nourish the body but also feed the soul, celebrating the cosmic dance through the flavors and rituals that connect us to the universe's vast and vibrant energy.

If you want to see some amazing products, please visit my Virtual Dispensary: https://shift.store/sg1fan23477/retail

Conclusion: Living in Harmony with the Stars

As we conclude our journey through "Zodiac Leaves: Aligning the Stars," it's important to reflect on the profound wisdom encapsulated within the cosmic dance of astrology and the earthy roots of herbalism. This ancient knowledge, when woven into the fabric of our daily lives, offers a rich tapestry of insights and practices that can guide us toward greater harmony, balance, and growth. The journey doesn't end here; rather, it unfolds with each day, inviting us to live more fully in alignment with the natural world and the celestial energies that influence it.

Integrating the Wisdom

The integration of astrology and herbalism into daily life is both an art and a science, requiring mindfulness, intuition, and a willingness to listen to the subtle cues of nature and the cosmos. Here are practical ways to bring this wisdom into your everyday experience:

- **Daily Rituals**: Begin each day with a ritual that connects you to the current astrological energies. This could be a simple meditation focused on the day's zodiac sign, a morning tea made from herbs aligned with that sign, or a few moments spent journaling intentions that resonate with the celestial influences at play.

- **Seasonal Celebrations**: Mark the turn of the astrological seasons by celebrating the ingress of the Sun into a new sign. Create feasts using ingredients that correspond to the sign, engage in rituals that honor its essence, and reflect on the themes it brings to your life.

- **Herbal Allies**: Cultivate a personal relationship with the herbs associated with your Sun, Moon, and Rising signs. Integrate these herbs into your cooking, teas, baths, or as part of your meditation practice. Let them be allies on your journey toward self-understanding and cosmic alignment.

- **Mindful Gardening**: If you have access to a garden space, consider creating a zodiac garden as a living, breathing space for meditation, reflection, and connection with the natural world. This garden can serve as a sanctuary where the cycles of life, reflected in both the botanical world and the stars, come into harmonious alignment.
- **Astrological Study**: Keep an astrological journal to track the Moon phases, planetary movements, and how they correlate with your personal experience. This practice can deepen your understanding of astrology's impact on your emotions, behaviors, and spiritual growth.

Continued Learning

The path of astrological herbalism is infinite, with each step revealing deeper layers of wisdom and insight. Encourage yourself to remain a perpetual student of the stars and the earth, exploring the following avenues for continued growth:

- **Educational Resources**: Seek out books, courses, and workshops that deepen your knowledge of astrology and herbalism. The learning journey is enriched by the wisdom of those who have walked the path before us.
- **Community Connection**: Join communities, both online and in-person, that share your interest in astrology and herbalism. These spaces offer support, inspiration, and the exchange of ideas that can propel your practice to new heights.
- **Personal Practice**: Develop a personal practice that blends astrological and herbal wisdom in a way that resonates with you. This could involve creating your own rituals, crafting herbal remedies, or simply observing the night sky with a sense of wonder and curiosity.
- **Teaching and Sharing**: As you gain knowledge and experience, consider sharing your insights with others. Teaching is not only

a powerful way to deepen your own understanding but also to spread the light of astrological herbalism further into the world.

Living in harmony with the stars and the earth is a journey of constant exploration, reflection, and growth. "Zodiac Leaves: Aligning the Stars" has offered a gateway into this rich and rewarding path. May you walk it with curiosity, openness, and a deep sense of connection to the cosmos that envelops us, the earth that sustains us, and the inner wisdom that guides us on our journey through life.

<u>Appendices</u>

Herbal Directory: Detailed Profiles for "Zodiac Leaves: Aligning the Stars"

This herbal directory serves as a comprehensive guide to the botanicals mentioned throughout "Zodiac Leaves: Aligning the Stars," offering insights into their astrological correspondences, medicinal properties, and practical uses. Each herb is a key to unlocking the wisdom of both the earth and the cosmos, aiding us in our journey towards harmony and balance.

1. Mugwort (Artemisia vulgaris)

Astrological Correspondence: Moon, Cancer **Uses**: Mugwort is revered for its dream-enhancing properties and its ability to open the doors of perception. It is often used in dream pillows or consumed as a tea to promote lucid dreaming and psychic exploration. Medicinally, it supports digestion and menstrual health.

2. Lavender (Lavandula angustifolia)

Astrological Correspondence: Mercury, Virgo **Uses**: Lavender is a calming herb that soothes the nervous system, promoting peace and relaxation. It is beneficial for treating anxiety, insomnia, and stress-related conditions. Lavender's pleasant fragrance also makes it a popular choice for aromatherapy and skin care products.

3. Chamomile (Matricaria chamomilla)

Astrological Correspondence: Sun, Leo **Uses**: Chamomile is known for its gentle, soothing effects, particularly beneficial for digestive discomfort and promoting restful sleep. Its anti-inflammatory and calming properties make it a staple in herbal medicine for treating a wide range of ailments.

4. Lemon Balm (Melissa officinalis)

Astrological Correspondence: Moon, Cancer **Uses**: Lemon balm uplifts the spirit, eases stress, and assists with anxiety and depression. It also helps with digestive issues and insomnia. This herb is often used in teas, culinary dishes, and as a topical treatment for herpes simplex virus.

5. Skullcap (Scutellaria lateriflora)

Astrological Correspondence: Saturn, Capricorn **Uses**: Skullcap is a nerve tonic that reduces anxiety, soothes nervous tension, and helps with sleep disorders. It is particularly useful for easing the symptoms of withdrawal from addictive substances.

6. Horsetail (Equisetum arvense)

Astrological Correspondence: Saturn, Capricorn **Uses**: Horsetail is rich in silica and supports bone health, hair, skin, and nail strength. It is also used as a diuretic and can aid in the healing of urinary tract infections and kidney stones.

7. Comfrey (Symphytum officinale)

Astrological Correspondence: Saturn, Capricorn **Uses**: Comfrey is known for its remarkable ability to heal broken bones, wounds, and bruises. Due to its high allantoin content, it accelerates cell regeneration but should be used with caution and never ingested due to its pyrrolizidine alkaloid content.

8. Nettle (Urtica dioica)

Astrological Correspondence: Mars, Aries **Uses**: Nettle is a nutritional powerhouse, rich in vitamins and minerals. It supports joint health, alleviates allergy symptoms, and is a tonic for the blood. Nettle can be consumed as a tea, in soups, or as a cooked green.

9. Dandelion (Taraxacum officinale)

Astrological Correspondence: Jupiter, Sagittarius **Uses**: Dandelion is a liver tonic that promotes detoxification and improves digestion. Both the root and the leaves are used medicinally, supporting kidney health, blood sugar regulation, and overall vitality.

10. Milk Thistle (Silybum marianum)

Astrological Correspondence: Jupiter, Sagittarius **Uses**: Milk thistle is best known for its protective and regenerative effects on the liver. It is used to treat liver disorders such as hepatitis and cirrhosis, as well as to protect the liver from damage by toxins or alcohol.

11. Turmeric (Curcuma longa)

Astrological Correspondence: Sun, Leo **Uses:** Turmeric is a potent anti-inflammatory and antioxidant herb, widely used to treat arthritis, digestive disorders, and skin conditions. It supports overall vitality and is a key ingredient in many culinary dishes for its color and flavor.

12. Ginger (Zingiber officinale)

Astrological Correspondence: Mars, Aries **Uses:** Ginger is a warming herb that aids digestion, relieves nausea, and combats inflammation. It is commonly used in cooking and can be taken as a tea, tincture, or supplement for its health benefits.

13. Passionflower (Passiflora incarnata)

Astrological Correspondence: Moon, Cancer **Uses:** Passionflower is a calming herb, ideal for treating anxiety, insomnia, and nervous disorders. It promotes relaxation without sedation, making it a valuable ally for those seeking a natural approach to stress relief.

14. Gotu Kola (Centella asiatica)

Astrological Correspondence: Moon, Cancer **Uses:** Gotu kola enhances cognitive function, supports wound healing, and improves circulation. It is often used in practices aimed at promoting longevity and spiritual development.

This herbal directory provides a starting point for incorporating astrological herbalism into your life. By engaging with these plants, whether through cultivation, culinary exploration, or ritualistic use, you invite the healing powers of the cosmos into your daily existence, fostering a deeper connection with the natural world and the stars that guide it.

Astrological Glossary for "Zodiac Leaves: Aligning the Stars"
The realm of astrology is rich with terminology that weaves together the tapestry of our cosmic narrative. This glossary serves as a key to unlocking the understanding of astrological terms and concepts used throughout "Zodiac Leaves: Aligning the Stars," offering clarity and insight into the celestial language that guides us.

A

- **Ascendant (Rising Sign)**: The zodiac sign that was rising on the eastern horizon at the moment of one's birth. It represents the personal façade, initial impressions, and physical appearance.
- **Aspect**: The angular relationship between planets in the natal chart, signifying how they interact with each other and influence the individual's personality and life events.

B

- **Birth Chart (Natal Chart)**: A map of where all the astrological elements were in their journey around the Sun (from our vantage point on earth) at the exact moment of one's birth.

C

- **Cardinal Signs (Aries, Cancer, Libra, Capricorn)**: Signs that initiate the seasons; known for leadership, initiative, and the drive to start new projects.

- **Conjunction**: An aspect in which two or more planets are positioned very closely together in the zodiac, blending and intensifying their energies.

D

- **Detriment**: A condition where a planet is positioned in the sign opposite to the one it rules, considered to weaken its influence.

E

- **Element**: The four basic building blocks of the universe reflected in astrology as Fire, Earth, Air, and Water, each associated with three zodiac signs.
- **Equinox**: The two times a year when day and night are of equal length, marking the beginning of spring and autumn.

F

- **Fixed Signs (Taurus, Leo, Scorpio, Aquarius)**: Signs known for stability, determination, and the ability to maintain and preserve.

H

- **House**: One of the twelve segments of the celestial sphere that make up the natal chart, each representing different areas of life.

I

- **Ingress**: The entry of a planet into a new sign, marking shifts in collective and personal energies.

M

- **Mutable Signs (Gemini, Virgo, Sagittarius, Pisces):** Signs that conclude the seasons; known for adaptability, flexibility, and change.

N

- **Natal Chart:** See Birth Chart.

O

- **Opposition:** An aspect where two planets are across from each other on the zodiac wheel, indicating challenges, tension, and the potential for integration.

P

- **Planetary Hours:** Segments of time in the day ruled by specific planets, each influencing different activities and energies.
- **Pluto:** The planet of transformation, power, and rebirth, associated with Scorpio.

R

- **Retrograde:** The apparent backward motion of a planet as seen from Earth, symbolizing a period of introspection and review in the areas ruled by the retrograding planet.

S

- **Saturn**: The planet of discipline, responsibility, and structure, associated with Capricorn.
- **Sign**: One of the 12 segments of the zodiac, each representing different personality traits, tendencies, and life themes.
- **Solstice**: The two times a year when the Sun reaches its highest or lowest point in the sky at noon, marking the beginning of summer and winter.
- **Square**: An aspect in which two planets are 90 degrees apart, indicating challenge, tension, and the potential for growth.

T

- **Trine**: An aspect where two planets are 120 degrees apart, signifying harmony, ease, and flow of energy.
- **Tropical Zodiac**: The zodiac system used in Western astrology, which is aligned with the Earth's seasons.

W

- **Water Signs (Cancer, Scorpio, Pisces)**: Signs associated with emotions, intuition, and the unconscious.

This glossary provides a foundational understanding of the astrological terms and concepts encountered in "Zodiac Leaves: Aligning the Stars." By familiarizing yourself with this language, you deepen your connection to the cosmic forces at play, enriching your journey through the wisdom of astrology and herbalism.

Resources: Further Reading and Exploration for "Zodiac Leaves: Aligning the Stars"

The journey through astrology and herbalism is rich and multifaceted, offering endless paths for exploration and growth. Whether you are a seasoned practitioner or a curious newcomer, the resources compiled here will guide you deeper into the realms of celestial wisdom and the healing power of the earth. These books, websites, and courses represent a wellspring of knowledge, ready to expand your understanding and practice of astrological herbalism.

Books on Astrology

1. **"The Only Astrology Book You'll Ever Need" by Joanna Martine Woolfolk**
   - A comprehensive guide that covers all the basics of astrology, including the signs, planets, houses, and aspects, making it an indispensable resource for beginners and seasoned astrologers alike.
2. **"Astrology for the Soul" by Jan Spiller**
   - This book offers a profound exploration of the North Node, providing insight into your soul's purpose and the growth opportunities present in your life.
3. **"Cosmos and Psyche: Intimations of a New World View" by Richard Tarnas**
   - Tarnas presents a compelling integration of astrology and psychology, exploring how planetary cycles correlate with historical events and personal transformation.

books on Herbalism

1. **"The Complete Herbs Sourcebook" by David Hoffmann**

- ° An extensive guide to herbal healing, covering hundreds of herbs, their uses, and detailed instructions for preparing herbal remedies.

2. **"Medical Astrology: Healing for the 21st Century" by Marcia Starck**
   - ° This book bridges the gap between astrology and herbalism, offering insights into how astrological conditions can influence physical health and how herbs can be used to balance these energies.

3. **"Braiding Sweetgrass" by Robin Wall Kimmerer**
   - ° While not exclusively about herbalism, this book beautifully weaves together indigenous wisdom, botany, and a deep reverence for the natural world, offering valuable insights for anyone interested in plant medicine.

Online Resources and Courses

1. **Astrodienst** (www.astro.com)
   - ° A comprehensive website offering free birth chart calculations, as well as articles and resources to deepen your understanding of astrology.

2. **The Herbal Academy** (www.theherbalacademy.com)
   - ° Offers a range of online courses and educational resources for herbalists of all levels, from beginners to advanced practitioners.

3. **Mountain Rose Herbs** (www.mountainroseherbs.com/blog)
   - ° An online herb supplier that also provides extensive educational content on herbalism, including how-to guides, recipes, and insights into the sustainable use of plant medicine.

Workshops and Events

- **United Astrology Conference (UAC)**

- ◦ A renowned international astrology conference that gathers experts from around the world, offering workshops, lectures, and networking opportunities for astrology enthusiasts.
- **HerbFest** (www.herbfest.net)
  - ◦ An annual event celebrating herbalism, with workshops, plant walks, and opportunities to learn from seasoned herbalists in a vibrant community setting.
- **Online Webinars and Workshops**
  - ◦ Many professional astrologers and herbalists offer webinars and online workshops. Platforms like Zoom and social media groups can be great places to find live events that resonate with your interests.

Embarking on a journey of learning in astrology and herbalism opens up a world of insight, healing, and connection to the natural cycles of the earth and sky. These resources are just the beginning, inviting you to explore the rich tapestry of knowledge that awaits. As you delve deeper into these studies, remember that the journey itself is as important as the destination, with each step revealing new layers of understanding and wonder.

<u>Message from the Author:</u>

I hope you enjoyed this book, I love astrology and knew there was not a book such as this out on the shelf. I love metaphysical items as well. Please check out my other books:

-Life of Government Benefits

-My life of Hell

-My life with Hydrocephalus

-Red Sky

-World Domination:Woman's rule

-World Domination:Woman's Rule 2: The War

-Life and Banishment of Apophis: book 1

-The Kidney Friendly Diet

-The Ultimate Hemp Cookbook

-Creating a Dispensary(legally)

-Cleanliness throughout life: the importance of showering from childhood to adulthood.

-Strong Roots: The Risks of Overcoddling children

-Hemp Horoscopes: Cosmic Insights and Earthly Healing

- Celestial Hemp Navigating the Zodiac: Through the Green Cosmos

-Astrological Hemp: Aligning The Stars with Earth's Ancient Herb

-The Astrological Guide to Hemp: Stars, Signs, and Sacred Leaves

-Green Growth: Innovative Marketing Strategies for your Hemp Products and Dispensary

-Cosmic Cannabis

-Astrological Munchies

-Henry The Hemp

-Zodiacal Roots: The Astrological Soul Of Hemp

- **Green Constellations: Intersection of Hemp and Zodiac**

-Hemp in The Houses: An astrological Adventure Through The Cannabis Galaxy

-Galactic Ganja Guide

Heavenly Hemp

Check out my Virtual dispensary for all your hemp needs: https://shift.store/sg1fan23477/retail

If you want solar for your home go here: https://www.harborsolar.live/apophisenterprises/

Instagrams: @apophis_enterprises, @hempkingdom2024, @apophisbookemporium, @apophisfashion, @apophisscardshop

Twitter: @apophisenterpr1, Tiktok:@apophisenterprise

Youtube: @sg1fan23477

Podcast: Apophis Chat Zone: https://open.spotify.com/show/5zXbrCLEV2xzCp8ybrfHsk?si=fb4d4fdbdce44dec

Newsletter: https://apophiss-newsletter-27c897.beehiiv.com/